U.S. PRESIDENTS
FEATS & FOUL-UPS

Jefferson

Washington

Jackson

Written by Nell Fuqua

Illustrated by Zina Saunders

Designed by Dan Jankowski

tangerine
press

an imprint of
SCHOLASTIC
www.scholastic.com

Scholastic and Tangerine Press and associated logos are trademarks of Scholastic Inc

Published by Tangerine Press, an imprint of Scholastic Inc; 557 Broadway; New York, NY 10012

10 9 8 7 6 5 4 3 2 1

ISBN 0-439-54081-X

Printed and bound in China

*T*he president of the United States is probably the most powerful person in the world. The president has to make decisions that affect both the United States and the rest of the planet. Sometimes it is very clear what the decision should be (such as ending slavery), but other times it is not so easy (such as going to war). After all, presidents are also people—and people are never perfect. We think of the presidents as being very intelligent and well-educated, having excellent social skills, and always being dignified. But just like other people, presidents also have hobbies, pets, favorite foods, nicknames, friends, enemies, triumphs, and embarrassing moments. This book takes a look at all the presidents: the great things they accomplished (feats), the mistakes (foul-ups) they made, and the silly events in their lives.

The Good

- Which president invented many labor-saving devices that we still use today?
- Who saved 77 swimmers from drowning?
- Who won a battle by partnering with French pirates?

The Bad

- Who thought he would be the last president of the United States?
- Which president gave up his United States citizenship?
- Who convinced Lincoln to exclude his home state from freeing its slaves?

The Silly

- Which president was offered a herd of elephants by the king of Siam?
- Which president liked to swim nude in the Potomac?
- Who had a birthday party for his dog?

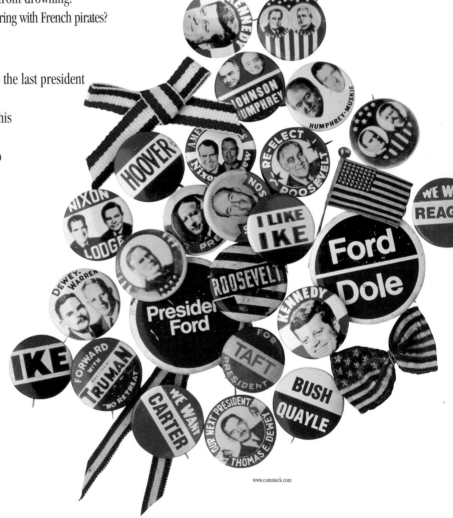

www.comstock.com

Read on to find out!

George Washington

Born:	February 22, 1732
Birthplace:	Westmoreland County, Virginia
College:	None
Religion:	Episcopalian
Profession:	Surveyor, Military, Planter
Political Party:	None
Term of office:	April 30, 1789 – March 3, 1797
Vice President:	John Adams
First Lady:	Martha Dandridge Custis Washington, his wife
Nickname:	Father of Our Country
Died:	December 14, 1799

"Observe good faith and justice toward all nations. Cultivate peace and harmony with all."

Firsts:

First president to appear on a postage stamp.

First man in American history to be a lieutenant general.

First six-star general, "General of the Armies of Congress," by an order of Jimmy Carter. Carter felt that America's first president should also be America's highest military official.

Feats:

- Became a land surveyor at age 15.
- Military spy for the British army at age 21.
- Member of the Virginia House of Burgesses.
- Commander in chief of the Continental army.
- President of the constitutional convention.
- Unanimously elected the country's first president (the only president ever elected unanimously).
- Established the precedent of controlling treaty negotiations, then asking for congressional approval.
- Established the precedent of remaining neutral regarding foreign quarrels.
- Refused to accept a crown and did not object to leaving office after two terms, setting an important precedent for limiting the president's power.
- Freed all his slaves (the only Founding Father to do so).

Foul-ups:

- Washington used to crack nuts with his teeth, according to John Adams. By the time he was elected president, he had only one natural tooth left in his mouth! Because of ill-fitting dentures, Washington's inauguration speech was 183 words long and took only 90 seconds to deliver.
- George Washington had to borrow money to attend his own inauguration.

Urban Legend:
Many people think Washington had wooden false teeth, but that's not true. He had a set of iron teeth, a set carved from ivory, and a set made from extracted human teeth!

Personal:

- Carried a portable sundial.
- Installed two ice cream freezers at his home, Mount Vernon.
- Fox hunting was his favorite sport.
- Had six white horses, whose teeth were brushed every morning on Washington's orders.
- Face scarred from smallpox.
- Left no direct descendants.

Feats:

- Successfully defended the British soldiers accused of murder in the Boston Massacre.
- Continental Congress.
- Commissioner to France.
- Minister to the Netherlands.
- Envoy to Great Britain.
- Vice president under George Washington.
- Signed new treaty with Napoleon Bonaparte, avoiding war with France.
- Created the Department of the Navy and organized the Marine Corps.

Firsts:

First president to live in the Executive Mansion (later called the White House).

First president whose son became president.

Foul-ups:

- Stole a sliver of wood from a chair at William Shakespeare's birthplace, as a souvenir.
- Led an unsuccessful effort in the Senate of the first Congress to make the office of president a royal, inherited position.
- When the Adamses moved into the White House, they discovered that the East Room was perfect for drying laundry.

Personal:

- As a boy, Adams hated studying Latin and asked his father for another "work" assignment. His father told him to try "ditching," by digging a ditch in a meadow. After two days, Adams happily went back to Latin.
- Adams died on July 4, 1826—the 50th birthday of the signing of the Declaration of Independence. He died within hours of his friend and former adversary, Thomas Jefferson. Adams lived longer than any president, and was 91 years old when he died.

John Adams

Born:	October 30, 1735
Birthplace:	Braintree, Massachusetts
College:	Harvard College
Religion:	Unitarian
Profession:	Teacher, Lawyer, Surveyor
Political Party:	Federalist
Term of Office:	March 4, 1797 – March 3, 1801
Vice President:	Thomas Jefferson
First Lady:	Abigail Smith Adams, his wife
Nickname:	Father of the American Navy
Died:	July 4, 1826

"I must study politics and war that my sons may have liberty to study mathematics and philosophy."

Thomas Jefferson

Born:	April 13, 1743
Birthplace:	Shadwell, Virginia
College:	College of William and Mary
Religion:	Deism (no formal affiliation)
Profession:	Lawyer, Planter
Political Party:	Democratic-Republican
Term of Office:	March 4, 1801 – March 3, 1809
Vice President:	Aaron Burr (1801 – 05), George Clinton (1805 – 09)
First Lady:	Martha "Patsy" Randolph, his daughter
Nickname:	Father of the Declaration of Independence
Died:	July 4, 1826

"In matters of principle, stand like a rock; in matters of taste, swim with the current."

Feats:

- Member of Virginia House of Burgesses.
- Continental Congress.
- Governor of Virginia.
- Minister to France.
- Wrote much of the Declaration of Independence.
- Secretary of state under George Washington.
- Vice president under John Adams.
- Bought the Louisiana Territory from France for $.04 per acre.
- Authorized the Lewis and Clark expedition.
- Founded the University of Virginia.
- Invented many devices (such as a swivel chair) that are still used today.

Firsts:

First president elected by the House of Representatives.

First president to shake hands instead of bow to people.

First president inaugurated in Washington, D.C.

Foul-ups:

- Called slavery an "abominable crime," but was a slaveholder all his life.
- Often greeted his dinner guests in old homespun clothes and a pair of worn bedroom slippers.

Personal:

- Had a pet mockingbird named Dick, who often rode on his shoulder .
- Played the violin.
- Took a cold foot bath every morning for 60 years.
- Once ate a tomato in public to prove it wasn't poisonous.
- Cultivated a garden and grew 15 varieties of his favorite vegetable, English peas.
- Believed that everyone should benefit from inventions that improve life, so never patented any of his inventions.

Feats:

- Graduated from Princeton University in only 2 years.
- Virginia House of Delegates.
- Continental Congress.
- U.S. House of Representatives.
- Co-authored the Federalist Papers.
- Secretary of state under Thomas Jefferson.
- Introduced the Bill of Rights to Congress.

Firsts:

Youngest member of the Continental Congress (age 29).

First president to wear long trousers.

First Easter Egg Roll on the Capitol grounds, started by Dolley Madison.

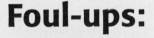

First presidential inaugural ball.

First time the Executive Mansion was called the White House.

Foul-ups:

- The young nation was not prepared for the War of 1812. The British entered Washington, D.C., and set fire to the White House.

Personal:

- Madison was the shortest president, at around 5 feet 4 inches.
- The "Star-Spangled Banner" was written during his presidency.
- Dolley Madison was criticized for gambling, wearing make-up, and using tobacco.
- Founding member of the American Colonization Society, which favored gradual abolition of slavery and resettlement of slaves and free blacks in Africa.

James Madison

Born:	March 16, 1751
Birthplace:	Port Conway, Virginia
College:	Princeton University
Religion:	Episcopalian
Profession:	Planter, Lawyer
Political Party:	Democratic Republican
Term of Office:	March 4, 1809 – March 3, 1817
Vice President:	George Clinton (1809-13), Elbridge Gerry (1813-17)
First Lady:	Dolley Payne Todd Madison, his wife
Nickname:	Father of the Constitution
Died:	June 28, 1836

4th

"The advice nearest to my heart and deepest in my convictions is, that the union of the states be cherished and perpetuated."

Feats:

- At age 15, looted a British arsenal and donated 200 muskets and 300 swords to the Virginia militia.
- Lieutenant colonel in the Continental army at age 20.
- Continental Congress.
- U.S. Senate.
- Minister to France.
- Governor of Virginia.
- Minister to Great Britain.
- Negotiated the Louisiana Purchase for Jefferson.
- Secretary of state under James Madison.
- Secretary of war under James Madison.
- Established the Monroe Doctrine, warning other nations not to interfere with any nation of the Western Hemisphere.
- Bought Florida from Spain.

Firsts:

Only president wounded in the Revolutionary War.

First president to ride on a steamboat.

First wedding ever performed in the White House, for daughter Marie Hester Monroe.

Foul-ups:

- Was recalled as Minister to France because he did not obey George Washington's orders.
- Voted against ratification of the U. S. Constitution because he wanted direct election of U.S. senators and president, and a strong bill of rights.

Personal:

- Spoke fluent French, and preferred it to English for personal conversation.
- Elizabeth Monroe saved the wife of the Marquis de Lafayette, as she awaited execution during the French Revolution.
- Was so popular that no one ran against him for re-election.

5th

James Monroe

Born:	April 28, 1758
Birthplace:	Westmoreland County, Virginia
College:	College of William and Mary
Religion:	Episcopalian
Profession:	Farmer, Lawyer, Military
Political Party:	Democratic-Republican
Term of Office:	March 4, 1817 – March 3, 1825
Vice President:	Daniel D. Tompkins
First Lady:	Elizabeth Kortright Monroe, his wife
Nickname:	The Last Cocked Hat
Died:	July 4, 1831

"The earth was given to mankind to support the greatest number of which it is capable, and no tribe or people have a right to withhold from the wants of others more than is necessary for their own support and comfort."

Feats:

- At age 14, went on a diplomatic mission to Russia.
- Minister to the Netherlands.
- Minister to Portugal.
- Minister to Prussia.
- U.S. Senate.
- Professor at Harvard College.
- Minister to Russia.
- Minister to Great Britain.
- Secretary of state under James Monroe.
- Author of the Monroe Doctrine.
- U.S. House of Representatives.

Firsts:

First president who was the son of a president.

First Minister to Russia.

First president to marry a foreign-born woman.

Foul-ups:

- Liked to take a nude swim in the Potomac, and once had to ask a passing stranger to bring him clothes from the White House when some boys stole the ones he had removed.
- Always left his fiancee's home before she and her sisters sang after dinner, because he hated the sound of women singing.

Personal:

- Installed the first billiard table in the White House.
- Kept a daily diary for 20 years.
- Helped establish the Smithsonian Institution.
- Louisa Adams, his wife, was born in England to an English mother and an American father.

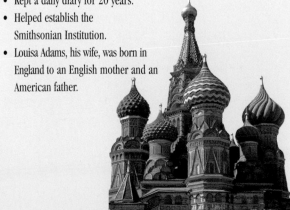

John Quincy Adams

Born:	July 11, 1767
Birthplace:	Braintree, Massachusetts
College:	Harvard College
Religion:	Unitarian
Profession:	Lawyer, College professor
Political Party:	Democratic-Republican
Term of Office:	March 4, 1825 – March 3, 1829
Vice President:	John C. Calhoun
First Lady:	Louisa Catherine Johnson, his wife
Nickname:	Old Man Eloquent
Died:	February 23, 1848

6th

"Slavery is the great and foul stain upon the North American Union..."

Andrew Jackson

Born:	March 15, 1767
Birthplace:	Waxhaw District, South Carolina
College:	None
Religion:	Presbyterian
Profession:	Lawyer, Military
Political Party:	Democratic
Term of Office:	March 4, 1829 – March 3, 1837
Vice President:	John C. Calhoun (1929-32), Martin Van Buren (1833-37)
First Lady:	Emily Donelson, niece of wife, Rachel
Nickname:	Old Hickory
Died:	June 8, 1845

"One man with courage makes a majority."

Feats:

- U.S. House of Representatives.
- Major general, defeated the British at the Battle of New Orleans.
- Governor of the Florida Territory
- U.S. Senate.

Firsts:

First president born in a log cabin.

First president to ride a railroad train.

First president nominated by a political party.

First president to survive an attempted assassination.

Only president to pay off the national debt.

Only president to be held as a prisoner of war (during the Revolutionary War, at age 13).

Only president to serve both in the Revolutionary War and the War of 1812.

Foul-ups:

- During Jackson's first inaugural celebration, his supporters overran the White House and tracked in mud, damaged furniture, tore the drapes, and started fights.
- Spent most of his adult life with a bullet lodged within two inches of his heart—the result of a duel he fought before becoming president.
- At Jackson's funeral in 1845, his pet parrot had to be removed because it was swearing.

Personal:

- At age 9, read newspapers to illiterate citizens and learned public speaking skills.
- At age 13, joined the army to fight the British and was captured.
- Caught smallpox while in prison, but recovered. However, his mother also caught the disease and died, leaving her son an orphan at the age of 14.
- In order to win the Battle of New Orleans, pardoned the French pirate Jean Lafitte. The British,who lost over 1,900 men, turned and fled. The Americans lost only 17 men.

Feats:

- Was a lawyer by age 20.
- U.S. Senate.
- Governor of New York.
- Secretary of state under Andrew Jackson.
- Minister to England.
- Vice president under Andrew Jackson.

Firsts:

First president born in the new United States.

Foul-ups:

- Only two months into his presidency, the country had an economic crisis known as the Panic of 1837. Interest rates skyrocketed, prices went up, people lost jobs, and food price riots broke out. But Van Buren continued to ride through Washington in an elegant coach pulled by matched horses, and attended by footmen dressed in fancy uniforms. The people thought he was a rich man who didn't care how hard their lives were.
- Opposed statehood for Texas and lost the support of Andrew Jackson.

- Ignored the Supreme Court's ruling and forced the removal of 20,000 Cherokee Indians from eastern states to Oklahoma. The forced march became known as the Trail of Tears, because over one quarter of the people died along the way.

Personal:

- Loved to dress in fine clothes, and the society section of the newspapers often described every detail of his appearance.
- His wife died, leaving him a widower with four sons to raise.

Martin Van Buren

Born:	December 5, 1782
Birthplace:	Kinderhook, New York
College:	None
Religion:	Dutch Reformed
Profession:	Lawyer
Political Party:	Democratic
Term of Office:	March 4, 1837 – March 3, 1841
Vice President:	Richard M. Johnson
First Lady:	Angelica Singleton Van Buren, his daughter-in-law
Nickname:	Little Magician
Died:	July 4, 1831

8th

"There is a power in public opinion in this country—and I thank God for it: for it is the most honest and best of all powers—which will not tolerate an incompetent or unworthy man to hold in his weak or wicked hands the lives and fortunes of his fellow-citizens."

William Henry Harrison

Born:	February 9, 1773
Birthplace:	Charles City County, Virginia
College:	Hampden-Sydney College; Philadelphia College of Physicians and Surgeons
Religion:	Episcopalian
Profession:	Planter, Military
Political Party:	Whig
Term of Office:	March 4, 1841 – April 4, 1841
Vice President:	John Tyler
First Lady:	Anna Tuthill Symmes Harrison, his wife (he died before his wife moved to Washington)
Nickname:	Old Tippecanoe
Died:	April 4, 1841

"There is nothing more corrupting, nothing more destructive of the noblest and finest feelings of our nature, than the exercise of unlimited power."

Feats:

- Territorial governor of Indiana.
- U.S. House of Representatives.
- U.S. Senate.
- Minister to Colombia.
- Defeated Tecumseh and the Shawnees at Tippecanoe Creek.

Firsts:

First Whig president.

First president to die in office.

First modern presidential campaign.

Foul-ups:

- At his inauguration, Harrison rode his horse in the parade even though it was cold and rainy. His inaugural speech was two hours long, and he did not wear a hat. He caught a cold that developed into pneumonia, and died after just 32 days in office.
- Opposed any attempt by Congress to restrict the spread of slavery or to limit the authority of slave masters over their slaves.
- While governor, Harrison made many treaties with the Native Americans that cheated them out of their lands for little money in return. In one case, he paid one penny for each 200 acres, and transferred 51 million acres to the United States.

Personal:

- Anna Symmes Harrison was the first. president's wife to have a formal education.
- He and his wife had 10 children.

Feats:

- U.S. House of Representatives.
- Governor of Virginia.
- U.S. Senate.
- Vice president under William Henry Harrison.
- Demanded that he be granted full presidential powers when Harrison died.
- Signed a treaty that opened up trade with China.

Firsts:

First vice president to become chief executive because the elected president died.

First president to be widowed and remarried while in office.

First president to have a veto overridden by Congress.

Only president to leave office without belonging to a political party.

Only president to give up his United States citizenship.

Foul-ups:

- Hired his oldest son as press secretary, but had to fire him for drinking too much.
- Was threatened with impeachment by both the Whigs and the Democratic party.
- Was elected in 1862 to the Confederate House of Representatives, and gave up his United States citizenship.

- Tyler's entire cabinet (expect for one man) resigned when he vetoed a bill to re-establish the Bank of the United States. Two days later, the Whigs demanded his resignation and expelled him from the party.

Personal:

- Had the most children of any president—15
- Tyler was born during George Washington's term, and his last child (fathered when Tyler was age 70) lived into the Truman presidency.
- Julia Tyler started the tradition of playing "Hail to the Chief" when the president entered the room.

John Tyler

10th

Born:	March 29, 1790
Birthplace:	Charles City County, Virginia
College:	College of William and Mary
Religion:	Episcopalian
Profession:	Lawyer, Planter
Political Party:	Whig (expelled in 1842)
Term of Office:	April 6, 1841 – March 3, 1845
Vice President:	None
First Lady:	Priscilla Cooper Tyler, his daughter-in-law; Julia Gardiner Tyler, his second wife
Nickname:	Accidental President
Died:	January 18, 1862

"The great primary and controlling interest of the American people is union—union not only in the mere forms of government . . . but union founded in an attachment of . . . individuals for each other."

Feats:

- U.S. House of Representatives.
- Speaker of the House of Representatives.
- Governor of Tennessee.
- Settled the Oregon border by a treaty with Great Britain.
- Won the Mexican War in 1848.
- Acquired Texas, California, Nevada, Colorado, New Mexico, Wyoming, Utah, and Arizona territories from Mexico (the most land acquired since the Louisiana Purchase).

Firsts:

First "dark horse" candidate of a party (a *dark horse* is a candidate nominated unexpectedly).

Only president to have been Speaker of the House.

First president not to seek re-election.

Foul-ups:

- Failed to do anything about social problems such as children working in factories, poverty of immigrants, and slavery.
- Sarah Polk replaced all White House servants with newly purchased slaves, whom she housed in the basement of the Executive Mansion in cramped sleeping quarters as a cost-saving measure.

Personal:

- At age 10, moved with his family by covered wagon to the frontier of Tennessee.
- At age 14, had abdominal surgery without anesthesia.
- Wore his hair long.
- Never had any children.
- Had few interests outside politics.
- Installed the first gas lighting in the White House, replacing oil and candles.

11th

James K. Polk

Born:	November 2, 1795
Birthplace:	Mecklenburg County, North Carolina
College:	University of North Carolina
Religion:	Presbyterian
Profession:	Store clerk, Lawyer
Political Party:	Democratic
Term of Office:	March 4, 1845 – March 3, 1849
Vice President:	George M. Dallas
First Lady:	Sarah Childress Polk, his wife
Nickname:	Young Hickory
Died:	June 15, 1849

"We must ever maintain the principle that the people of this continent alone have the right to decide their own destiny."

Feats:

- Defeated Mexican General Santa Anna with a much smaller army and became a national hero.
- Never lost a battle.

Firsts:

First president not previously elected to any public office.

Foul-ups:

- Refused to engage Congress in a debate over slavery.
- Failed to solve the problem of whether to admit new western states as slave or free states.
- Never voted, never belonged to a political party, and never took interest in politics until he ran for president at age 62.

Personal:

- Was short and had to be boosted into his saddle.
- Was an unusual dresser, and often mixed military and civilian dress.
- Taylor's wife made a vow not to go into society if her husband returned safely from the Mexican War. That's why Taylor's daughter, Betty, assumed the role of first lady.
- Taylor's oldest daughter, Sara, married one of his officers from the Mexican War—Lt. Jefferson Davis. Davis later became president of the Confederacy.
- Died of cholera after serving only 16 months in office.
- At Taylor's funeral, the presidential hearse was drawn by eight white horses accompanied by grooms dressed in white and wearing white turbans. It was followed by Washington dignitaries, military units, the president's beloved horse, Old Whitey, and the president's family.

*Poster of Zachary Taylor on his horse, Old Whitey

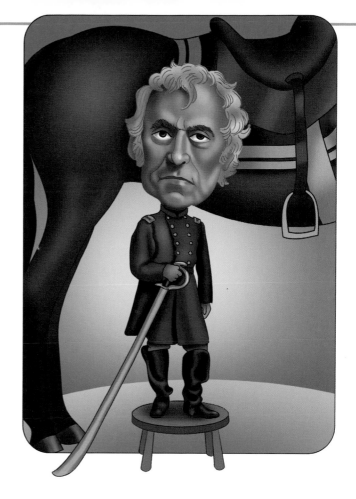

Zachary Taylor

Born:	November 24, 1784
Birthplace:	Orange County, Virginia
College:	None
Religion:	Episcopalian
Profession:	Military
Political Party:	Whig
Term of Office:	March 4, 1849 – July 9, 1850
Vice President:	Millard Fillmore
First Lady:	Betty Taylor Bliss, his daughter
Nickname:	Old Rough and Ready
Died:	July 9, 1850

12th

"My life has been devoted to arms, yet I look upon war at all times and under any circumstances as a national calamity to be avoided if compatible with National Honor..."

Millard Fillmore

Born:	January 7, 1800
Birthplace:	Cayuga County, New York
College:	None
Religion:	Unitarian
Profession:	Apprentice to cloth dresser and wool carder, Military, Lawyer
Political Party:	Whig
Term of Office:	July 10, 1850 – March 3, 1853
Vice President:	None
First Lady:	Abigail Fillmore, his wife
Nickname:	The Compromise President
Died:	March 8, 1874

"God knows that I detest slavery, but it is an existing evil, for which we are not responsible, and we must endure it, till we can get rid of it without destroying the last hope of free government in the world."

Feats:

- U.S. House of Representatives.
- Vice president under Zachary Taylor.
- Signed the Compromise of 1850, keeping America from civil war for over ten years.

Firsts:

First White House library started.

First president to send a trade commission to Japan.

Foul-ups:

- Sought the Whig nomination for president after completing Taylor's term, but did not receive it.
- Fillmore ended his career heading the Know-Nothings, a party formed to oppose immigration.

Personal:

- Fillmore's family was desperately poor. His father apprenticed him to a clothmaker who made him work 15 hours a day. Fillmore finally managed to borrow thirty dollars and pay his obligation to the clothmaker. Free, he walked one hundred miles to get back home to his family.
- Taught himself to read.
- Fillmore was 18 years old when he started school. He married his teacher, Abigail Powers, who was only two years older than he was.
- Brought the first cast iron stove to the White House, replacing the fireplace.
- Installed the first bathtub with running water in the White House.
- Fillmore was a founding member and president of the Buffalo chapter of the American Society for the Prevention of Cruelty to Animals.

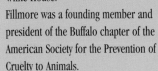

Feats:

- U.S. House of Representatives.
- U.S. Senate.
- Brigadier general during the Mexican War.
- Gadsden Purchase acquired border lands from Mexico.

Firsts:

First president born in the 19th century.

Only president to have said "I promise" instead of "I swear" at his inauguration (for religious reasons).

First president to introduce the Christmas tree to the White House.

Only president to keep all members of his cabinet for four years.

Only elected president who was not renominated by his party for a second term.

Foul-ups:

- As an inexperienced young general in the Mexican War, Pierce had a terrible accident on his horse that crushed his leg. Because he fainted from the accident, and because his men had no respect for his military skills, Pierce acquired the unfortunate nickname, "Fainting Frank."
- Had a reputation for drinking and partying during his early years in Congress.
- Often called on Varina Davis (wife of his secretary of war, Jefferson Davis) to act as hostess because of the first lady's poor health and depression (Davis later became president of the Confederacy!).

Personal:

- Was a classmate of Nathaniel Hawthorne and Henry Wadsworth Longfellow.
- Pierce did not run for president. His Democratic friends nominated him, but he never made even one campaign speech.

Franklin Pierce

Born:	November 23, 1804
Birthplace:	Hillsborough, New Hampshire
College:	Bowdoin College
Religion:	Episcopalian
Profession:	Lawyer, Military
Political Party:	Democratic
Term of Office:	March 4, 1853 – March 3, 1857
Vice President:	William R. D. King
First Lady:	Jane Appleton Pierce, his wife
Nickname:	Fainting Frank
Died:	October 8, 1869

"I believe that involuntary servitude [slavery], as it exists in different States of this Confederacy, is recognized by the Constitution."

Feats:

- U.S. House of Representatives.
- Minister to Russia.
- U.S. Senate.
- Secretary of state under James K. Polk.
- Minister to England.

Firsts:

Only president to have never married.

First cable message sent across the Atlantic Ocean from Queen Victoria of England to President Buchanan.

Foul-ups:

- Ran for the presidency four times before finally winning.
- South Carolina, Mississippi, Florida, Alabama, Georgia, Louisiana, and Texas seceded and formed the Confederate States of America. Buchanan did nothing to stop them.
- Because of the Civil War, Buchanan actually believed he would be the last president of the United States.

Personal:

- Was engaged to a wealthy young woman, but her family opposed the marriage. Upon her sudden death, he was not allowed to attend the funeral and vowed never to marry. Though he carried on many flirtations, he was never seriously involved with another woman the rest of his life.
- Even though he was a bachelor, Buchanan loved entertaining. Aided by his beautiful and popular niece, Harriet Lane, Buchanan sponsored endless dances and parties at the White House.
- The king of Siam offered to send him several pairs of elephants that could be "turned loose in forests and increase till there be large herds." The offer was later politely declined by Abraham Lincoln.

15th

James Buchanan

Born:	April 23, 1791
Birthplace:	Cove Gap, Pennsylvania
College:	Dickinson College
Religion:	Presbyterian
Profession:	Lawyer
Political Party:	Democratic
Term of Office:	March 4, 1857 – March 3, 1861
Vice President:	John C. Breckinridge
First Lady:	Harriet Lane, his niece
Nickname:	Old Buck
Died:	June 1, 1868

"My dear, sir, if you are as happy on entering the White House as I on leaving, you are a very happy man indeed."

(to Abraham Lincoln)

Abraham Lincoln

Born:	February 12, 1809
Birthplace:	Hardin County, Kentucky
College:	No formal education
Religion:	No formal membership
Profession:	Farm hand, Boatman, Lawyer, Postmaster, Surveyor
Political Party:	Republican
Term of Office:	March 4, 1861 – April 15, 1865
Vice President:	Hannibal Hamlin (1861-65), Andrew Johnson (March 4 – April 15, 1865)
First Lady:	Mary Todd Lincoln, his wife
Nickname:	The Great Emancipator
Died:	April 15, 1865

GETTYSBURG ADDRESS

Firsts:

First president born outside the original thirteen colonies.

First Republican president.

First use of income tax.

First use of "greenbacks"—paper money not redeemable for gold or silver.

First use of the draft to supply men for the army.

Only president to obtain a patent.

First president to be assassinated.

"It is true that you may fool all the people some of the time; you can even fool some of the people all the time; but you cannot fool all of the people all the time."

Feats:

- U.S. House of Representatives.
- Delivered the Gettysburg Address, one of the greatest speeches in American history, while suffering from smallpox.
- Supported the Homestead Act of 1862, which gave 160 acres to any adult who claimed and lived on the land for five years.
- Signed a law that gave land to the states to develop universities.
- Issued the Emancipation Proclamation, freeing 3 million slaves.
- Preserved the Union.
- Chosen by historians as the nation's greatest president.

*Lincoln's Emancipation Proclamation was issued on January 1, 1863

Urban Legend:

Lincoln did not write the Gettysburg Address on the back of an envelope while traveling by train from Washington, D.C. He worked on the address both before and after his trip to Gettysburg, using official stationery for part of the speech. The train ride would have been too bumpy to do any writing.

Foul-ups:

- In 1842, Lincoln was challenged to a duel. Since he was challenged, he had the privilege of naming the conditions for the contest. He proposed the outrageous spectacle of a fight with cavalry broad swords while standing in a square ten feet wide and twelve feet deep, which would have put the much shorter man at a huge disadvantage. He probably thought this silly idea would bring the challenger to his senses. Both men prepared for the duel until their *seconds* ("assistants" who came along for support) managed to arrange a peaceable settlement.

- After Lincoln made him the military governor of Tennessee, Andrew Johnson convinced the president to exempt Tennessee from the Emancipation Proclamation.

- Asked Robert E. Lee to command the Union army, but Lee offered his services to the Confederacy instead.

- At the end of the Civil War, Lincoln requested that a band play "Dixie!" He said it was one of his favorite songs, and that he had "fairly captured it."

- As a first-term Whig congressman, he condemned the War of 1812 as an unconstitutional and aggressive act, a position so unpopular with his constituents that he decided not to run for a second term.

Personal:

- At age 19, Lincoln built a flatboat and ran a load of farm produce down the Mississippi River from Illinois to New Orleans. Selling the boat for its timber, he then walked home via the Natchez Trace and gave his full earnings to his father.
- Wrestling was one of his favorite sports.
- While Lincoln was campaigning for president, an 11-year-old girl suggested that he grow a beard because his face was so thin. She said a beard would make him more appealing, and that "all the ladies like whiskers." He took her advice, and the rest is history!
- Was the tallest president, at 6 feet 4 inches.
- Was an excellent marbles player, and played for relaxation during the Civil War.
- Assassinated by John Wilkes Booth, 5 days after ending the war.

Feats:

- U.S. House of Representatives.
- Governor of Tennessee.
- U.S. Senate.
- Military governor of Tennessee.
- Vice president under Abraham Lincoln.
- Purchased Alaska from Russia for $.02 per acre (negotiated by Secretary of State William Seward, and known as "Seward's icebox").

Firsts:

Only southern senator not to resign his seat during the Civil War.

First president impeached; acquitted in the Senate by only one vote.

First president to be visited by a queen, Queen Emma of the Sandwich Islands (Hawaii).

Only former president elected to the U.S. Senate.

Foul-ups:

- Did not master the basics of reading or math until he was age 18 (his future wife taught him).
- Vetoed Congressional bills to:
  - enforce political and civil rights for southern blacks
  - provide shelter and provision for ex-slaves and protection of their rights in court
  - define all people born in the U.S. as citizens
  - protect the rights of all citizens
  - limit the president's power to remove federal officials without Senate approval.

  However, Congress passed each of these bills over his veto.

Personal:

- Apprenticed to a tailor at age 14, Johnson ran away and dodged rewards for his capture posted by his employer. He returned to his family a couple of years later, and they moved to Tennessee.
- Designed and made some of his own clothes.
- Johnson's wife was an invalid, so his married daughter served as official hostess.
- Johnson left flour out at night for a family of mice playing in his room during his dark days of impeachment.

Andrew Johnson

Born:	December 29, 1808
Birthplace:	Raleigh, North Carolina
College:	No formal education
Religion:	No formal membership
Profession:	Tailor
Political Party:	Democratic
Term of Office:	April 15, 1865 – March 3, 1869
Vice President:	None
First Lady:	Martha Johnson Patterson, his daughter
Nickname:	None
Died:	July 31, 1875

"If the rabble were lopped off at one end and the aristocrat at the other, all would be well with the country."

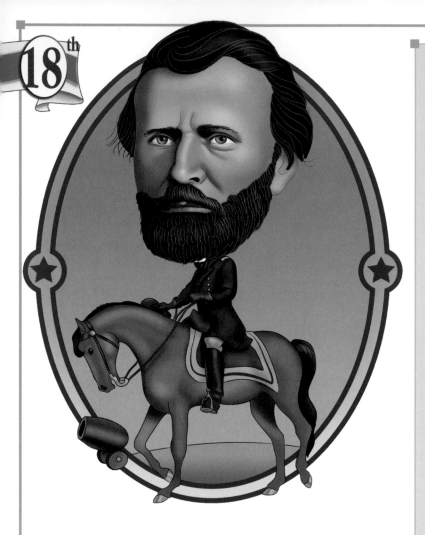

Ulysses S. Grant

Born:	April 27, 1822
Birthplace:	Point Pleasant, Ohio
College:	U.S. Military Academy at West Point
Religion:	Methodist
Profession:	Military, Farmer, Business
Political Party:	Republican
Term of Office:	March 4, 1869 – March 3, 1877
Vice President:	Schuyler Colfax (1869-73),
	Henry Wilson (1873-75)
First Lady:	Julia Dent Grant, his wife
Nickname:	Hero of Appomattox
Died:	July 23, 1885

"Social equality is not a subject to be legislated upon."

Feats:

- Commander of the Union armies during the Civil War.
- Wrote generous terms of surrender at Appomattox Courthouse, preventing treason trials for Confederates.
- Secretary of war under Andrew Johnson.
- Passed the 15th Amendment, which gave all qualified male citizens the right to vote.

Firsts:

First transcontinental railroad completed.

First president elected in part by former slaves.

First president to have a woman run against him in a campaign.

Foul-ups:

- Forced to resign his army commission because of excessive drinking.
- Received a $20 ticket for speeding his carriage through Washington, D.C.
- Did not include women in the rights bestowed by the 15th Amendment.
- Appointed friends to his cabinet, who turned out to be incompetent and corrupt.
- Smoked 20 cigars a day, and died from throat cancer.

Personal:

- Completed his memoirs just two days before he died from throat cancer. The book was published with help from Mark Twain, and the royalties took care of his family.
- Was an accomplished horseman.

Feats:

- At age 40, joined the Union army during the Civil War and rose to rank of major general.
- U.S. House of Representatives.
- Governor of Ohio.
- Restored dignity and respect to the office of the president after Lincoln's assassination, Johnson's impeachment, and Grant's corrupt administration.
- Vetoed a bill that would have ended Chinese immigration, pointing out that it violated a treaty obligation.

Firsts:

First president to graduate from law school.

First president to have a telephone in the White House (installed by Alexander Graham Bell).

First president's wife to be called "first lady."

First first lady to graduate from college.

First president to travel to the West Coast.

Foul-ups:

- Ended Reconstruction, allowing the Democratic Party to sweep in and dominate the region. The Democratic hold on the South resulted in a complete denial of rights for blacks, including the right to vote, for nearly a century.

Personal:

- Offered refuge and free legal assistance to escaped slaves.
- Did not drink or smoke in an era that saw almost every other man doing so.
- Refused a desk job during the Civil War, and was wounded five times.
- Won the presidential election by only one electoral vote.
- Lucy Hayes was nicknamed "Lemonade Lucy" because she refused to serve alcohol at White House functions.
- In 1877, the president and his wife celebrated their silver wedding anniversary by renewing their vows before scores of lifelong friends at the White House.
- Had the first Siamese kitten in the United States.

Rutherford B. Hayes

Born:	October 4, 1822
Birthplace:	Delaware, Ohio
College:	Kenyon College, Harvard Law School
Religion:	No formal affiliation
Profession:	Lawyer
Political Party:	Republican
Term of Office:	March 4, 1877 – March 3, 1881
Vice President:	William A. Wheeler
First Lady:	Lucy Ware Webb Hayes, his wife
Nickname:	Dark-Horse President
Died:	January 17, 1893

"It is now true that this is God's Country, if equal rights—a fair start and an equal chance in the race of life are everywhere secured to all."

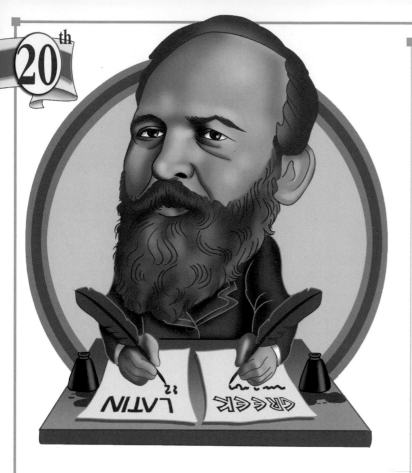

James A. Garfield

Born: November 19, 1831
Birthplace: Orange, Ohio
College: Williams College
Religion: Disciples of Christ
Profession: Canal bargeman, Teacher, Carpenter, Lawyer
Political Party: Republican
Term of Office: March 4, 1881 – September 19, 1881
Vice President: Chester A. Arthur
First Lady: Lucretia Rudolph Garfield, his wife
Nickname: Preacher President
Died: September 19, 1881

"A brave man is a man who dares to look the Devil in the face and tell him he is a Devil."

Feats:

- At age 26, became president of Hiram College.
- U.S. House of Representatives.
- U.S. Senate.
- Ended the military occupation of the South.
- Served as a regent of the Smithsonian Institution.

Firsts:

First president to campaign in two languages: English and German.

First left-handed president.

Foul-ups:

- When he was 16, Garfield ran away to work on the canal boats that shuttled between Cleveland and Pittsburgh. During the six weeks he worked on the boats, he fell overboard 14 times and finally got so sick he had to return home.

Personal:

- Of all the presidents, Garfield came from the poorest family.
- Could write Latin with one hand and Greek with the other.
- As a presidential candidate, Garfield addressed an assembly of German speakers in their native language.
- Mrs. Garfield caught malaria from the swamps behind the White House, but made a full recovery.
- Garfield was shot in the back by Charles Julius Guiteau, an emotionally disturbed man who had failed to gain an appointment in Garfield's administration. Repeated probing for the bullet with non-sterile instruments led to blood poisoning, which eventually killed Garfield.

Feats:

- Quartermaster general of New York.
- Vice president under James Garfield.
- Reformed civil service by making government jobs competitive and requiring a written test.
- Modernized the navy by building steel ships (known as "Father of the Steel Navy").

Firsts:

First president to hire a *valet* (a servant who performs personal services, such as taking care of clothing).

Foul-ups:

- Suspended as Collector of the Port of New York by President Rutherford B. Hayes (who thought Arthur had used the tax money to reward his political supporters).
- Vetoed the Chinese Exclusion Act of 1882, which banned all Chinese immigration into the U.S. for ten years. The veto was overridden by Congress.

Personal:

- Had over 80 pairs of pants, and changed clothes several times a day.
- Hired the most famous designer in New York, Louis Tiffany, to refurnish the White House.
- Fishing was his favorite activity.
- Arthur first refused to move into the White House, describing it as "a badly kept barracks." He had twenty-four wagonloads of furniture removed before having it redecorated.
- Hired a French gourmet chef to take charge of the White House kitchen.

Chester A. Arthur

21st

Born:	October 5, 1829
Birthplace:	Fairfield, Vermont
College:	Union College
Religion:	Episcopalian
Profession:	Teacher, Lawyer
Political Party:	Republican
Term of Office:	September 20, 1881 – March 3, 1885
Vice President:	None
First Lady:	Mary Arthur McElroy, his sister
Nickname:	Gentleman Boss
Died:	November 18, 1886

"No higher or more assuring proof could exist of the strength and permanence of popular government than the fact that though the chosen of the people be struck down, his constitutional successor is peacefully installed without shock or strain . . ."

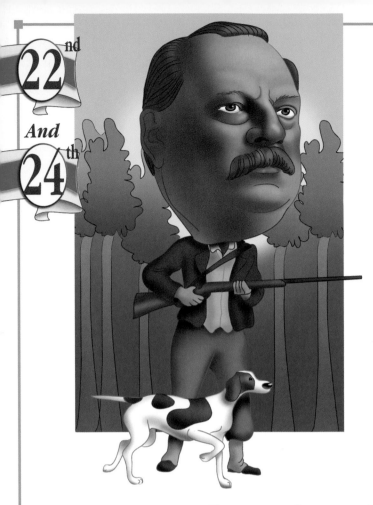

Grover Cleveland

Born:	March 18, 1837
Birthplace:	Caldwell, New Jersey
College:	None
Religion:	Presbyterian
Profession:	Lawyer, Sheriff
Political Party:	Democratic
Term of Office:	March 4, 1885 – March 3, 1889; March 4 1893 – March 3, 1897
Vice President:	Thomas A. Hendricks (1885-89), Adlai E. Stevenson (1893-97)
First Lady:	Frances Folsom Cleveland, his wife
Nickname:	Big Steve
Died:	June 24, 1908

"It is the responsibility of the citizens to support their government. It is not the responsibility of the government to support its citizens."

Feats:

- Mayor of Buffalo, NY.
- Governor of New York.

Firsts:

Only president to serve two non-consecutive terms.

Only president married in the White House.

First child born in the White House (his second child, Esther).

First president to deliver his inaugural address without notes.

Foul-ups:

Queen Liliuokalani

- Tried to give Hawaii back to Queen Liliuokalani, because he believed the revolution of 1893 was a conspiracy by American sugar planters and President Harrison's foreign office. He gave up when she refused to pardon the revolutionary leaders (she wanted them beheaded) and the sugar planters threatened armed resistance.
- Cleveland, an avid hunter and outdoorsman, disappeared with some friends into the Adirondack Mountains, without indicating where they were going. When they did not return after several days, rumors circulated that they were lost.
- Used federal troops to suppress labor unrest during the Panic of 1893.

Personal:

- Avoided being drafted into the Union army by hiring a substitute for $300.
- Married a woman who was 27 years younger, the daughter of his former law partner.
- Became a trustee of Princeton University.

Feats:

- Brigadier general in the Union army.
- U.S. Senate.
- Appointed former slave Frederick Douglass as ambassador to Haiti.
- Added six new states: North Dakota, South Dakota, Montana, Washington, Idaho, and Wyoming—more than any other president.

Firsts:

First president to install electricity in the White House.

First Pan-American Conference (encouraged good will between the U.S. and Latin America).

Last Civil War general to become president.

First grandson of a president (William Henry Harrison) to become president.

Foul-ups:

- Tried to add Hawaii as a state after white settlers overthrew Queen Liliuokalani, but the Senate did not approve.
- After installing electric lighting, the Harrisons were afraid to touch the switches, so they left the lights on all night.
- Shot a farmer's pig by mistake, while hunting.

Personal:

- Spent as little time as possible in the office, usually working only until noon.
- Hated small talk, so those who met him thought he was cold and aloof.
- Mrs. Harrison died right before the end of her husband's term. After leaving the presidency, Harrison remarried and had a daughter who was younger than his grandchildren.

Benjamin Harrison

Born:	August 20, 1833
Birthplace:	North Bend, Ohio
College:	Miami University of Ohio
Religion:	Presbyterian
Profession:	Lawyer
Political Party:	Republican
Term of Office:	March 4, 1889 – March 3, 1893
Vice President:	Levi P. Morton
First Lady:	Caroline Lavinia Scott Harrison, his wife
Nickname:	Human Iceberg
Died:	March 13, 1901

"I believe also in the American opportunity which puts the starry sky above every boy's head, and sets his foot upon a ladder which he may climb until his strength gives out."

William McKinley

Born:	January 29, 1843
Birthplace:	Niles, Ohio
College:	Allegheny College, Albany Law School
Religion:	Methodist
Profession:	Teacher, Lawyer
Political Party:	Republican
Term of Office:	March 4, 1897 – September 14, 1901
Vice President:	Garrett Hobart (1897-99), Theodore Roosevelt (March 4 – Sept. 14, 1901)
First Lady:	Ida Saxton McKinley, his wife
Nickname:	Wobbly Willie
Died:	September 14, 1901

"We want no war of conquest . . .
War should never be entered upon
until every agency of peace has failed."

Feats:

- U.S. House of Representatives.
- Governor of Ohio.
- Entered the Spanish-American War after the sinking of the U.S. battleship *Maine* in Cuba, and won.
- Acquired the Philippines, Puerto Rico, Guam, and American Samoa.
- Annexed Hawaii.

Firsts:

First international war with a European power (Spain) since the War of 1812.

First used the telephone for campaign purposes.

First president to ride in an automobile (the ambulance that took him to the hospital after he was shot).

Foul-ups:

- Raised tariffs on imported goods to an all-time high, making them the largest source of government income.
- Did little to help black Americans secure the right to vote and become politically active.

Personal:

- Served on the staff of Colonel Rutherford B. Hayes, future president of the United States, during the Civil War.
- His trademark pink carnation always decorated his lapel, and he liked giving it to acquaintances as a personal token of his affection.
- Invited the nation's press to regular briefings, establishing the forerunner of the presidential press conference.
- Asassinated by Leon F. Czolgosz, an unemployed mill worker.

Theodore Roosevelt

Born:	October 27, 1858
Birthplace:	New York, New York
College:	Harvard College
Religion:	Dutch Reformed
Profession:	Author, Lawyer
Political Party:	Republican
Term of office:	September 14, 1901 – March 3, 1909
Vice President:	Charles W. Fairbanks
First Lady:	Edith Carow Roosevelt, his wife
Nickname:	Teddy
Died:	January 6, 1919

Firsts:

First environmentalist president.

First president to be photographed in action.

Youngest man ever to hold the office of president.

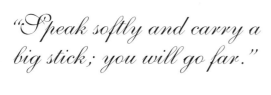

"Speak softly and carry a big stick; you will go far."

"Do what you can, with what you have, where you are."

Feats:

- Commander of Rough Riders.
- Assistant secretary of the navy.
- Governor of New York.
- Vice president under McKinley.
- Started the Panama Canal.
- Nobel Peace Prize.
- Congressional Medal of Honor.
- Set aside over 230 million acres for national forests, reserves, parks, and refuges.
- Established the National Wildlife Refuge Program.
- Wrote over 30 books.
- Wounded in the chest by a would-be assassin's bullet, but delivered an eloquent campaign speech for 90 minutes before being rushed to a hospital.

Foul-ups:

- Lost the election for mayor of New York City.
- During a boxing match, he suffered a detached retina that blinded him in that eye.
- His six children took their pony, Algonquin, into the White House elevator, frightened visiting officials with a four-foot King snake, and dropped water balloons onto the heads of the White House guards.
- After losing the election in 1912, he went on safari in Africa and bagged over 3,000 animal trophies–including elephants, hippos, lions, and rhinos.

Protected lands

Roosevelt wanted to save the nation's wilderness regions because he believed they had helped shape American values, culture, and behavior. The amount of area that he protected is greater than France, Belgium, and the Netherlands combined. Among the many areas he saved are:

Grand Canyon	**Crater Lake**
Mesa Verde	**Muir Woods**
Montezuma's	**Black Hills**
Castle	**Natural Bridges**
Petrified Forest	**Mount Olympus**

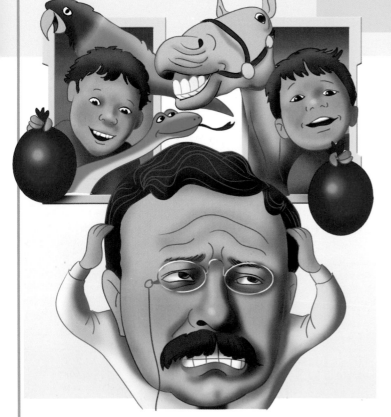

Personal:

- As a boy, Roosevelt was frail and sickly. As a teenager, he developed a rugged physique and became a life-long advocate of excercise and the "strenuous life."
- His first wife, Alice Lee, and his mother both died on the same day, in the same house. He spent two years in North Dakota to recover from the tragedy, and worked as a cattle rancher and deputy sheriff.
- The "Teddy bear" was named for him, after he refused to shoot a bear cub that had been tied to a tree.

Feats:

- Civil governor of the Philippines.
- Secretary of war under Theodore Roosevelt.
- Supervised construction of the Panama Canal.
- Extended statehood to Arizona and New Mexico.
- Chief justice of the Supreme Court.

Firsts:

First president to open the baseball season by throwing out the "first pitch."

First president to take up golf.

Only man to hold both the highest executive office (president) and the highest judicial office (chief justice of the Supreme Court).

First president to be buried at Arlington National Cemetery.

Foul-ups:

- Taft so disappointed his predecessor and former mentor that Roosevelt bolted from the Republican party to form his own "Bull-Moose" party.
- Got stuck in the White House bathtub, and needed six men to pull him out.
- He frequently embarrassed his family and associates by falling asleep at concerts, during presidential briefing sessions, while presiding over his cabinet, and just about anytime and anywhere.

Personal:

- He was the largest president, weighing over 300 pounds.
- His love of golf caused a boom in the sport across the nation.
- Mrs. Taft fell in love with the cherry trees she saw during a trip to Japan, and had three thousand Japanese cherry trees sent to Washington, D.C. Every spring these trees still delight visitors to the city.
- Taft was the last president to keep a cow on the White House lawn. She lived in the garage, with the president's automobiles.

27th

William H. Taft

Born: September 15, 1857
Birthplace: Cincinnati, Ohio
College: Yale College
Religion: Unitarian
Profession: Lawyer
Political Party: Republican
Term of Office: March 4, 1909 – March 3, 1913
Vice President: James S. Sherman
First Lady: Helen "Nellie" Herron Taft, his wife
Nickname: Big Bill
Died: March 8, 1930

"We live in a stage of politics, where legislators seem to regard the passage of laws as much more important than the results of their enforcement."

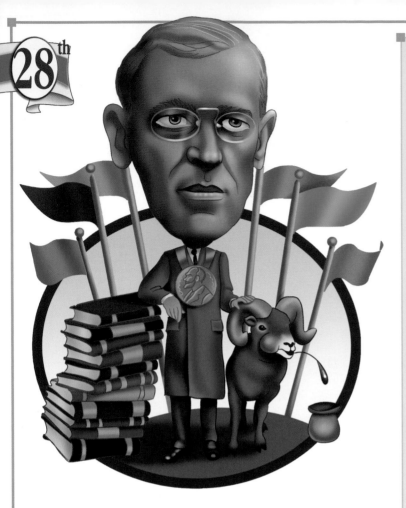

Woodrow Wilson

Born:	December 28, 1856
Birthplace:	Staunton, Virginia
College:	College of New Jersey
	(now Princeton University);
	Johns Hopkins University
Religion:	Presbyterian
Profession:	Lawyer, Professor, Author,
	College president
Political Party:	Democratic
Term of Office:	March 4, 1913 – March 3, 1921
Vice President:	Thomas R. Marshall
First Lady:	Ellen Axson Wilson (1913-14);
	Edith Galt Wilson (1916-21),
	his wives
Nickname:	None
Died:	February 3, 1924

*"I believe in democracy because it releases
the energies of every human being."*

Feats:

- President of College of New Jersey (now Princeton University).
- Governor of New Jersey.
- Established a bill of rights for the Philippines and territorial independence for Puerto Rico.
- Entered World War I when the Germans refused to stop their submarine warfare after 120 Americans were killed aboard the British liner, *Lusitania*, and a secret correspondence between Germany and Mexico was uncovered.
- Ended child labor.
- Proposed the League of Nations as part of his peace plan following World War I.
- Negotiated 22 international treaties.
- Purchased the Virgin Islands from Denmark.
- Won the Nobel Peace Prize.

Firsts:

First president to travel to Europe while in office.

First president to appoint a Jewish justice to the Supreme Court.

Foul-ups:

- Sent U.S. forces into Mexico on an unsuccessful mission to try to get a change of government.
- Sponsored the Espionage and Sedition Acts, which outlawed criticism of the government, the armed forces, and the war effort (violators of the law were imprisoned or fined, mainstream publications were censored or banned).
- America never joined the League of Nations, because Wilson refused to compromise with the Senate.

Personal:

- Because of manpower shortage during the war, Wilson replaced White House gardeners with sheep. They kept the grass trimmed, and he donated their wool to the Red Cross for soldiers' uniforms. Among the sheep was an old ram named Old Ike, who chewed tobacco.
- Edith Wilson was a descendant of Pocahontas.
- Suffered a stroke and saw no one but his wife during the final months of his presidency.

Feats:

- U.S. Senate.
- Held a conference with nine other nations to freeze naval spending in an effort to reduce taxes.
- Mrs. Harding enlisted several previous first ladies to help in her campaign to aid veterans (they were known as "Flossie's Gang").

Firsts:

First president to have a radio in the White House.

First president to broadcast a presidential message by radio.

First president to ride to his inauguration in an automobile.

First president for whom women could vote.

Foul-ups:

- Missed many important senate sessions because he wanted to avoid arguments.
- Gambled away the White House china in a card game.
- Appointed several trusted friends to the cabinet (the "Ohio gang"), who took bribes and stole money from the government. Harding's secretary of the interior went to jail because he took bribes and granted oil leases to Wyoming's Teapot Dome.
- Served alcohol to his friends, even though Prohibition made it illegal.

Personal:

- Liked to play poker, smoke, drink whiskey, play golf, and keep late hours
- Threw a birthday party for his dog, Laddie Boy, and invited all the neighborhood dogs. The cake had many layers of dog biscuits. Newsboys donated pennies to make a statue of Laddie Boy, which now stands in the Smithsonian Institution.
- Laddie Boy (an Airedale terrier of impeccable reputation) was more popular with the press than Harding. On July 17, 1921, the *Washington Star* printed an "interview" with Laddie Boy in which he gave his opinion on everything from Woodrow Wilson's sheep and Prohibition to the Harding cabinet, and he advocated an eight-hour day for guard dogs.

Warren Harding

Born:	November 2, 1865
Birthplace:	(near) Corsica, Ohio
College:	Ohio Central College
Religion:	Baptist
Profession:	Editor/publisher
Political Party:	Republican
Term of Office:	March 4, 1921 – August 2, 1923
Vice President:	Calvin Coolidge
First Lady:	Florence Kling De Wolfe Harding, his wife
Nickname:	None
Died:	August 2, 1923

"Our most dangerous tendency is to expect too much of government, and at the same time do for it too little."

Feats:

- Governor of Massachusetts.
- Vice president under Harding.
- Grace Coolidge brought national attention to the plight of the nation's hearing-impaired, and became a close personal friend of Helen Keller.

Firsts:

First president sworn into office by his father.

First president sworn into office by a former president (Taft, during his second inauguration).

Foul-ups:

- Kept all of Harding's cabinet, including scandal-plagued Attorney General Harry M. Daugherty.
- Refused to allow Mrs. Coolidge to wear pants or culottes.
- Vetoed a farm relief bill that might have prevented the Great Depression.

Personal:

- After the death of Warren Harding in 1923, Coolidge was sworn in by his father, a justice of the peace, and promptly went back to bed.
- Was silent in cabinet meetings, and rarely spoke in the Senate, thus earning the nickname "Silent Cal."
- Coolidge was a highly visible leader, holding press conferences, speaking on the radio, and posing for portraits dressed in farmer overalls, cowboy hats and chaps, and full Indian headdresses.
- Loved to smoke expensive Cuban cigars.
- Installed a mechanical horse in the White House.
- He had many pets, but a racoon named Rebecca was his favorite. He built a special house for her, visited her every day, and walked her around the White House on a leash.

30th

Calvin Coolidge

Born:	July 4, 1872
Birthplace:	Plymouth, Vermont
College:	Amherst College
Religion:	Congregationalist
Profession:	Lawyer
Political Party:	Republican
Term of Office:	August 3, 1923 – March 3, 1929
Vice President:	Charles G. Dawes
First Lady:	Grace Anna Goodhue Coolidge, his wife
Nickname:	Silent Cal
Died:	January 5, 1933

"This country would not be a land of opportunity, America would not be America, if the people were shackled with government monopolies."

Feats:

- Chairman of European Relief Council.
- Secretary of commerce under Harding and Coolidge.
- Coordinator of Food Supply for World Famine.
- Raised over 1 billion dollars for food and medicine to aid Europe after World War I.
- Accepted no salary for his term, and assigned the presidential yacht to the navy.
- Received over 50 honorary degrees from American universities, and over 25 honorary degrees from foreign universities.

Firsts:

First president born west of the Mississippi River.

First asteroid named for a president: *Hooveria*.

First president visited by an absolute monarch (King Prajadhipok of Siam).

Foul-ups:

- Hoover refused to help the unemployed or feed the hungry after the New York Stock Market crashed on October 29, 1929. Nearly 2 million men, women and children roamed the nation, riding the rails and living as "hoboes" in dirty shantytowns called "Hoovervilles." For warmth, they wrapped themselves in newspapers, or "Hoover blankets," and the jackrabbits they ate were called "Hoover hogs."
- During his bid for reelection, his train was pelted with tomatoes and eggs by people in the Midwest.
- Unemployment increased 149%, and over 100,000 Americans applied for work in the Soviet Union.

Personal:

- Often spoke Chinese with the first lady when they wanted to avoid being overheard .
- Was a millionaire by age 40, from high-paying jobs, a silver mine, and royalties from a textbook on mining.
- Loved to fly-fish in remote streams.
- Traveled the world with his wife and discovered gold in Australia and China.

31st

Herbert Hoover

Born:	August 10, 1874
Birthplace:	West Branch, Iowa
College:	Stanford University
Religion:	Society of Friends (Quaker)
Profession:	Mining engineer, Author
Political Party:	Republican
Term of Office:	March 4, 1929 – March 3, 1933
Vice President:	Charles Curtis
First Lady:	Lou Henry Hoover, his wife
Nickname:	The Great Engineer
Died:	October 20, 1964

"Prosperity cannot be restored by raids upon the public treasury."

Franklin Delano Roosevelt

Born:	January 30, 1882
Birthplace:	Hyde Park, New York
College:	Harvard College, Columbia Law School
Religion:	Episcopalian
Profession:	Lawyer, Author
Political Party:	Democratic
Term of Office:	March 4, 1933 – April 12, 1945
Vice President:	John Garner (1933-37), Henry Wallace (1937-41), Harry S. Truman (1941-45)
First Lady:	Anna Eleanor Roosevelt, his wife
Nickname:	FDR
Died:	April 12, 1945

"We have nothing to fear but fear itself."

Firsts:

Only president to be elected to four terms.

First president to appoint a woman to a cabinet position.

First president to appoint a woman (Ruth Bryan Owen) as minister to a foreign country, (Denmark and Iceland).

First president to visit South America while in office.

First president to visit Hawaii while in office.

First president to appear on television.

First president to broadcast in a foreign language (French).

Feats:

- Assistant secretary of the navy.
- Governor of New York.
- During the "First Hundred Days" of his term, pushed through legislation to reform banking, subsidize agriculture, and help businesses.
- Started New Deal programs that brought relief to thousands of unemployed and hungry people.
- Declared war on Japan after Pearl Harbor was bombed.
- Guided America through World War II, it's greatest foreign crisis, and the Great Depression, its greatest domestic crisis (except for the Civil War).
- Reassured the nation with his "fireside chats," using the new medium of radio.
- Created Social Security to provide pensions for the elderly and to aid the disabled.

Foul-ups:

- Ordered the internment of 110,000 mainland Americans of Japanese ancestry in guarded relocation camps, many of them in the desert.
- Created TVA (Tennessee Valley Authority) to provide cheap electricity for rural areas, but it became the biggest polluter of the natural environment.
- Attempted to increase the number of judges on the Supreme Court, but Congress rebelled.
- Had to banish his German shepherd, Major, for biting guests and ripping the pants of the British prime minister.

Personal:

- FDR was related to 11 presidents and 13 passengers on the *Mayflower.*
- At age 5, FDR met Grover Cleveland. The president said, "My little man, I am making a strange wish for you. It is that you will never be president of the United States."
- FDR and Eleanor were fifth cousins, and Eleanor was Teddy Roosevelt's niece.
- Stricken with polio in 1921, FDR was unable to walk unassisted for the rest of his life.
- Hid his disability so well that many Americans never knew he was confined to a wheelchair.
- Was sworn in on a Dutch bible that had been his family for three centuries.
- Fala, a black Scottish terrier, was his favorite pet and went everywhere with him.
- Was an avid stamp collector, and acquired over 25,000 stamps.

Feats:

- U.S. Senate.
- Vice president under FDR.
- Hastened the end of World War II by dropping atomic bombs on Japan.
- Ended segregation in the armed services.
- Sent American troops to South Korea to keep the Communists from taking it.

Firsts:

Only 20th-century president not to have a college education.

First president to present a medal of honor to a conscientious objector (a medic on Okinawa) for heroism.

First president to travel underwater on a modern submarine.

First president to officially receive a woman ambassador from a foreign country (India).

First former president to address the Senate (on his 80th birthday).

Foul-ups:

- A piano leg went through the rotten floor of the White House.
- His daughter, Mary Margaret, was an opera singer who didn't always get good reviews. Truman sometimes wrote angry letters to her critics.

Personal:

- Read all the books in his local library by age 14.
- Was an artillery officer during World War I.
- Married his childhood sweetheart.
- Became president after being vice president for only 82 days, when FDR died.
- Was an excellent pianist and brought three pianos to the White House.
- Dismissed General Douglas MacArthur for not obeying orders.
- Favorite saying: "If you can't stand the heat, get out of the kitchen."
- Had dozens of tailor-made suits, which showed off his trim physique.

33rd

Harry S. Truman

Born:	May 8, 1884
Birthplace:	Lamar, Missouri
College:	University of Kansas City Law School
Religion:	Baptist
Profession:	Farmer, Store owner, Judge
Political Party:	Democratic
Term of Office:	April 12, 1945 – January 20, 1953
Vice President:	John Garner (1945-49), Alben Barkley (1949-53)
First Lady:	Elizabeth "Bess" Virginia Wallace Truman, his wife
Nickname:	Give 'em Hell Harry
Died:	December 26, 1972

"Within the first few months, I discovered that being a president is like riding a tiger. A man has to keep on riding or be swallowed."

Feats:

- Supreme Commander of Allied Expeditionary Forces.
- Chief of Staff.
- President of Columbia University.
- Supreme Commander of NATO.
- His Interstate Highway Act (1956) provided for a 41,000-mile interstate highway system, the single largest public works program in American history.
- Ended the Korean War by negotiating a cease-fire in which Korea was divided at the 38th parallel.
- Built the St. Lawrence Seaway in partnership with Canada.

Firsts:

Only president to serve in both World War I and World War II.

First president to ride in a nuclear submarine.

First president to have a pilot's license.

First president to fly in the presidential jet.

Foul-ups:

- Was injured trying to tackle Olympic medalist Jim Thorpe in a college football game.
- Allowed corporations to use the toxic chemical DDT, resulting in the poisoning of people and wildlife.
- Remained silent when Senator Joseph McCarthy was at the height of his power, abusing the civil liberties of hundreds of citizens whom the senator accused of anti-American activities.
- Did not back up the Supreme Court's ruling to desegregate schools.
- Banished squirrels from the White House grounds because they were destroying his golf green.

Personal:

- His mother, Ida, a Mennonite, was a religious pacifist who opposed war and violence of any kind.
- After retiring, enjoyed painting by numbers.
- Installed a golf green on White House grounds.
- Changed the name of Shangri-La, the presidential retreat, to Camp David (in honor of his grandson).

Dwight D. Eisenhower

34th

Born:	October 14, 1890
Birthplace:	Denison, Texas
College:	U.S. Military Academy, West Point
Religion:	Presbyterian
Profession:	Military
Political Party:	Republican
Term of Office:	January 20, 1953 – January 20, 1961
Vice President:	Richard M. Nixon
First Lady:	Mary "Mamie" Geneva Doud Eisenhower, his wife
Nickname:	Ike
Died:	March 28, 1969

"What counts is not necessarily the size of the dog in the fight—it's the size of the fight in the dog."

Feats:

- Naval commander in World War II.
- Won the Pulitzer Prize.
- U.S. House of Representatives.
- U.S. Senate.
- Founded the Peace Corps.
- Supported the space program with a pledge to put Americans on the moon by the end of the decade.
- Prevented war with the Soviet Union by agreeing to remove American missiles in Turkey if the Soviets removed their missiles in Cuba.
- Signed an agreement with the Soviet Union and Great Britain that limited the testing of nuclear weapons.

Firsts:

Youngest man ever elected president, at age 43.

First president born in the 20th century.

First televised presidential debates (with Richard Nixon).

Foul-ups:

- Had one of the worst attendance records in Congress, due to his poor health.
- Proclaimed his solidarity with the people of Berlin, Germany, saying "Ich bin ein Berliner." He meant to say that he was a Berliner along with them, but actually said that he was a "cake," because "berliner" in German refers to a popular dessert.

Personal:

- The large Kennedy family was known for playing touch football on the White House lawn.
- Tormented by back trouble, malaria, and Addison's disease, Kennedy was administered his Last Rites (the Catholic prayer for the dying) at least four times during his life.
- During World War II, Kennedy's PT Boat 109 was rammed by a Japanese destroyer. He led the crew's ten survivors on a three-mile swim to a tiny island. He received U.S. Navy and Marine Corps Medals for valor, and a Purple Heart for injuries.
- Assassinated after just 1,000 days in office, by Lee Harvey Oswald.

35th

John F. Kennedy

Born:	May 29, 1917
Birthplace:	Brookline, Massachusetts
College:	Harvard College
Religion:	Roman Catholic
Profession:	Military, Author, Newspaper correspondent
Political Party:	Democratic
Term of Office:	January 20, 1961 – November 22, 1963
Vice President:	Lyndon B. Johnson
First Lady:	Jacqueline Bouvier Kennedy, his wife
Nickname:	JFK
Died:	November 22, 1963

"And so, my fellow Americans: ask not what your country can do for you— ask what you can do for your country."

Feats:

- U.S. House of Representatives.
- U.S. Senate.
- Vice president under John Kennedy.
- Created Medicare, a program providing federal funding of many healthcare expenses for senior citizens.
- His Great Society program established environmental protection laws, highway safety laws, and money to promote the arts.
- His War on Poverty funded Head Start early education programs, legal aid for the poor, and job training.
- Proposed the Voting Rights Act, which opened the voting process to African-Americans.

Firsts:

Only president sworn into office on an airplane.

First president to appoint an African-American cabinet member.

First president to nominate an African-American to the Supreme Court.

Foul-ups:

- Did poorly in school, and was not admitted into college on his first attempt.
- Was arrested for fighting before he was accepted into college.
- Increased American military support in Vietnam to 500,000, but still couldn't win the war.

Personal:

- Proposed to Lady Bird the day after they met (married three months later).
- All members of his family had the initials "LBJ."
- Johnson's mongrel dog, Yuki, "sang" duets with the president, appeared on the front page of the *Wall Street Journal*, and bit a White House police officer.

Lyndon B. Johnson

Born:	August 27, 1908
Birthplace:	Stonewall, Texas
College:	Southwest Texas State Teachers College; Georgetown Law School
Religion:	Disciples of Christ
Profession:	Teacher
Political Party:	Democratic
Term of Office:	November 22, 1963 – January 20, 1969
Vice President:	Hubert H. Humphrey
First Lady:	Claudia "Lady Bird" Alta Taylor Johnson, his wife
Nickname:	LBJ
Died:	January 22, 1973

"We have talked long enough in this country about equal rights. We have talked for one hundred years or more. It is time now to write it in the books of law."

37th

Richard Nixon

Born: January 9, 1913
Birthplace: Yorba Linda, California
College: Whittier College;
Duke University Law School
Religion: Society of Friends (Quaker)
Profession: Lawyer
Political Party: Republican
Term of Office: January 20, 1969 – August 9, 1974
Vice President: Spiro T. Agnew
(January 20, 1969 –
October 10, 1973);
Gerald R. Ford
(December 6, 1973 – August 9, 1974)
First Lady: Thelma "Patricia" Catherine
Ryan Nixon, his wife
Nickname: Tricky Dick
Died: April 22, 1994

*"This office is a sacred trust and I am determined
to be worthy of that trust."*

Feats:

- Naval officer during World War II.
- U.S. House of Representatives.
- U.S. Senate.
- Vice president under Dwight Eisenhower.
- Ended America's role in Vietnam.
- Opened talks with China and exchanged "ping-pong" teams to promote goodwill.
- Created the Environmental Protection Agency.

Firsts:

First president to travel to the Soviet Union.

First president to travel to China.

Only president to resign his office.

Foul-ups:

- Rejected by the FBI when he applied to become an agent after college.
- Lost his bid to become governor of California.
- Lost the 1960 presidential election to Kennedy.
- Developed a reputation for running incorrect "attack" ads against his competitors, often accusing them of being "soft on communism." One of his opponents called him "Tricky Dick" for doing this, and the nickname stuck.
- During his presidential re-election campaign, Nixon allowed advisors to do many illegal things to stay ahead of the Democrats. When they were caught breaking into the Democratic national headquarters at the Watergate apartment complex, Nixon's staff tried to cover up the incident. This made the American public angry, and Nixon resigned before he could be impeached.
- Spiro Agnew, his vice president, resigned when he was proven to have taken bribes.

Personal:

- Was an excellent poker player.
- Met his future wife when both joined a community theater group.
- Liked to play the piano, and would invite guests to sing along.
- His youngest daughter, Julie, married David Eisenhower, one of President Eisenhower's grandsons.

Feats:

- Won ten battle stars as a Naval officer during World War II.
- U.S. House of Representatives.
- House Minority Leader.
- Vice president under Nixon.
- Presidential Medal of Freedom (awarded by President Clinton, in honor of his public service in binding the nation together after the Watergate scandal).
- Presidential Medal of Freedom awarded to Mrs. Ford (awarded by President George Bush in honor of her outstanding work in drug and alcohol rehabilitation).

Firsts:

First president never elected to the executive branch (became vice president when Agnew resigned, after being nominated by Nixon and approved by Congress).

First president to hire a professional joke writer.

Foul-ups:

- Pardoned Nixon, making many voters angry.
- While campaigning for re-election in the southwestern United States, he attempted to eat Mexican tamales without first removing the cornhusks.
- After a stumble was captured on camera, he had a reputation as a "klutz."

Personal:

- Had offers from the Detroit Lions and the Green Bay Packers to play professional football.
- During college, worked at Yellowstone Park and as a male model.
- Was in excellent physical condition, and was one of the most athletic of all presidents.
- In 1975, survived two assassination attempts—both by women (who were sent to prison for life).
- When Oval Office meetings lasted too long, he used Liberty, his golden retriever, to break things up.

Gerald Ford

Born:	July 14, 1913
Birthplace:	Omaha, Nebraska
College:	University of Michigan; Yale University Law School
Religion:	Episcopalian
Profession:	Lawyer
Political Party:	Republican
Term of Office:	August 9, 1974 – January 20, 1977
Vice President:	Nelson A. Rockefeller
First Lady:	Elizabeth "Betty" Bloomer Ford, his wife
Nickname:	Jerry

"If the government is big enough to give you everything you want, it is big enough to take away everything you have."

Jimmy Carter

Born:	October 1, 1924
Birthplace:	Plains, Georgia
College:	U.S. Naval Academy
Religion:	Baptist
Profession:	Military, Farmer, Author
Political Party:	Democrat
Term of Office:	January 20, 1977 – January 20, 1981
Vice President:	Walter F. Mondale
First Lady:	Eleanor Rosalynn Smith Carter, his wife
Nickname:	Jimmy

"A strong nation, like a strong person, can afford to be gentle, firm, thoughtful, and restrained. It can afford to extend a helping hand to others. It's a weak nation, like a weak person, that must behave with bluster and boasting and rashness and other signs of insecurity."

Feats:

- Governor of Georgia.
- Negotiated the Camp David Accords—an historic peace agreement between Israel and Egypt.
- Established a "superfund" to clean up environmental disasters.
- Established excellent trade relations with China.
- Gave control of the Panama Canal back to Panama.
- Helped found Habitat for Humanity, which builds homes for poor people.
- Won the Nobel Peace Prize.

Firsts:

First president born in a hospital.

First president to serve as an officer on a nuclear submarine.

First president sworn in using his nickname.

Foul-ups:

- Boycotted the 1980 Summer Olympics, which were held in Moscow, to protest the Soviet invasion of Afghanistan. Many people thought this act punished American athletes more than Soviet leaders.
- Iranian militants stormed the U.S. embassy in Teheran and took about 70 hostages. Carter sent American troops to rescue them, but the mission failed.
- Largest inflation increase since 1946.

Personal:

- Grew up in a home that did not have electricity or indoor plumbing.
- Built a tree house on the White House grounds for his daughter, Amy.
- Carter has served as a freelance ambassador for a variety of international missions, including soothing disputes between countries, observing elections in nations with histories of fraudulent voting processes, and advising presidents on Middle East issues.
- In 2002, he won the Nobel Peace Prize for his humanitarian efforts.

Feats:

- As a lifeguard, saved 77 people.
- Appeared in over 50 movies.
- Governor of California.
- Congressional Medal of Honor, jointly with his wife, Nancy.
- Signed a treaty with the Soviet Union to limit the nuclear arms race.
- Achieved the biggest tax cuts in U. S. history.

Firsts:

First president who had been a Hollywood actor.

First president to be head of a labor union (Screen Actors Guild).

First president to appoint a woman, Sandra Day O'Connor, to the Supreme Court.

Foul-ups:

- Married his first wife, Jane Wyman, at Forest Lawn Cemetery in Glendale, California.
- Oversaw the accumulation of more new debt than all previous presidents added together.
- Members of his administration made secret, illegal deals to give weapons to Iran in exchange for American hostages.

Personal:

- The Jelly Belly® brand created the blueberry flavor especially for him so that red, white, and blue jelly beans could be served at his inaugural party.
- Rancho del Cielo is the name of his ranch. The name means "farm of the sky."
- He was the oldest man elected president (at age 69).
- Survived an assassination attempt by John Hinckley, a mentally disturbed man.

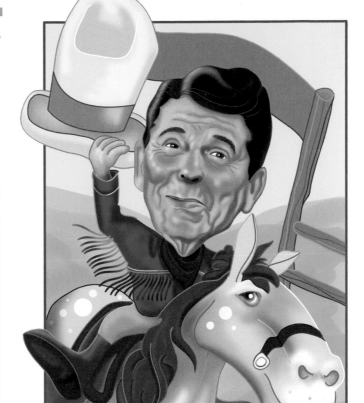

Ronald Reagan

Born: February 6, 1911
Birthplace: Tampico, Illinois
College: Eureka College
Religion: Disciples of Christ
Profession: Sports announcer, Actor
Political Party: Republican
Term of office: January 20, 1981 – January 20, 1989
Vice President: George H.W. Bush
First Lady: Nancy Davis Reagan, his wife
Nickname: The Great Communicator

40th

"America is too great for small dreams."

Feats:

- Received Distinguished Flying Cross and three air medals as a pilot in World War II.
- U.S. House of Representatives.
- U.S. ambassador to the United Nations.
- U.S. envoy to China.
- Director of the Central Intelligence Agency (CIA).
- Vice president under Ronald Reagan.
- Pushed Iraqi dictator, Saddam Hussein, out of Kuwait during the Persian Gulf War.

Firsts:

First president who had been head of the CIA.

First president who had been ambassador to the United Nations.

Foul-ups:

- Raised taxes, after saying, "Read my lips, no new taxes."
- Raised only a mild objection when China sent tanks and soldiers against students in Beijing.
- Did not remove Saddam Hussein from power after the success of the Persian Gulf War.

Personal:

- Was related to four previous presidents.
- Enlisted at age 18, and became the youngest pilot in the navy when he received his wings in 1943.
- Played baseball at Yale and kept a first-baseman's glove in his desk in the Oval Office.
- Started his own oil business in Texas and became wealthy.
- Challenged Russian leader, Mikhail Gorbachev, to a game of horseshoes—and Gorbachev threw a "ringer" (when the horseshoe encircles the post) on his first toss .
- Hated broccoli so much that he banished it from the White House.

George Bush

Born:	June 12, 1924
Birthplace:	Milton, Massachusetts
College:	Yale University
Religion:	Episcopalian
Profession:	Business
Political Party:	Republican
Term of Office:	January 20, 1989 – January 20, 1993
Vice President:	J. Danforth Quayle
First Lady:	Barbara Pierce Bush, his wife
Nickname:	Poppy

"America is never wholly herself unless she is engaged in high moral principle. We as a people have such a purpose today. It is to make kinder the face of the nation and gentler the face of the world."

** www.comstock.com

Feats:

- Attended Oxford University in London as a Rhodes Scholar.
- Governor of Arkansas.
- Negotiated peace in Northern Ireland between Protestants and Catholics.
- Directed peace talks between Israel and the Palestine Liberation Organization (PLO).
- Negotiated the North American Free Trade Agreement (NAFTA) with Canada and Mexico.
- Led U.S. allies in forcing Serbia to stop attacking Muslims in Bosnia.
- Turned the biggest budget deficit in history into a surplus.

Firsts:

Youngest governor in the nation and the youngest in Arkansas history, at age 32.

Foul-ups:

- Lost his first bid for re-election as governor.
- His universal health care plan, led by Mrs. Clinton, was not approved by Congress.
- Impeached by the House of Representatives on charges of lying under oath and obstructing justice (was not convicted by the Senate).

Personal:

- Started collecting books about the presidents as a child.
- As a 17-year-old delegate to Boys' Nation, he met President Kennedy and had his picture taken while shaking the president's hand.
- Participated in many demonstrations against the Vietnam War, while at Oxford.
- An excellent saxophone player, he once considered becoming a professional musician.
- Had a Labrador retriever named Buddy, and a cat named Socks.
- Loves fast food.
- Was nicknamed "Slick Willy" because he often changed his mind on issues.

Bill Clinton

Born:	August 19, 1946
Birthplace:	Hope, Arkansas
College:	Georgetown University, Yale University Law School
Religion:	Baptist
Profession:	Professor, Lawyer
Political Party:	Democrat
Term of Office:	January 20, 1993 – January 20, 2001
Vice President:	Al Gore
First Lady:	Hillary Rodham Clinton, his wife
Nickname:	Slick Willy

"If you live long enough, you'll make mistakes. But if you learn from them, you'll be a better person. It's how you handle adversity, not how it affects you. The main thing is never quit, never quit, never quit."

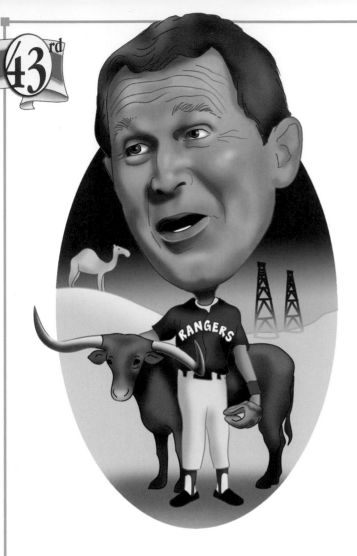

George W. Bush

Born:	July 6, 1946
Birthplace:	New Haven, CT
College:	Yale University; Harvard University
Religion:	Methodist
Profession:	Business
Political Party:	Republican
Term of Office:	January 20, 2001 – present
Vice President:	Dick Cheney
First Lady:	Laura Welch Bush, his wife
Nickname:	Dubya ("W")

"I was not elected to serve one party, but to serve one nation."

Feats:

- Governor of Texas.
- Raised more than $36 million for his presidential campaign in the first six months of 1999—a new record.
- Passed a bill that cut every American's taxes.
- Established a new cabinet office for Homeland Security, as a result of the terrorist attacks on New York City on September 11, 2001.
- Organized a war against terrorists.

Firsts:

Longest presidential election, with closest outcome in history.

First presidential election outcome appealed to the U.S. Supreme Court.

First president to appoint an African-American as secretary of state.

Foul-ups:

- Once repaired his broken bed with neckties.
- Drove his car into the garage wall when his wife criticized a speech he had just made.
- Air quality in Texas became one of the worst in the nation while he was governor.
- Won the electoral votes, but trailed his opponent by nearly 1½ million popular votes.

Personal:

- Head football cheerleader his senior year in high school.
- Married his wife three months after meeting on a date arranged by friends.
- Twin daughters, Barbara and Jenna, are named for their grandmothers.
- Managing partner and part owner of Texas Rangers baseball team,1989-1998.
- Has a pet longhorn cow named Ofelia.
- Has collected over 250 autographed baseballs.
- His ranch is known as the "Texas White House," or the "Western White House."